For Hazel

3

Bolt Down This Earth

Gram ~~Joel~~ Davies

24/5/17

V.

Published in the United Kingdom in 2017
by V. Press,
10 Vernon Grove,
Droitwich,
Worcestershire,
WR9 9LQ.

ISBN: 978-0-9926114-9-1

Cover image © Gram Joel Davies, 2017

Cover design © Ruth Stacey, 2017

Printed in the U.K. by Imprint Digital, Seychelles Farm, Upton Pyne, Exeter EX5 5HY, on recycled paper stock.

V.

Contents

V.

V.

How Can I Mourn a Man Still Living?

At the edge of my ears, a single nerve
rings like a tungsten bulb.

All I have done is mention the orchard
where my dad would take us to buy from a man
who measured sugar into cider flagons.
Through planted rows awash
with a slow syrup of photons, I hear
the apple fallout of the branches.

Only a mention—but my dad looks to have witnessed
a flash over the horizon. A bottled
ferment from his centre rushes
staggered trees.

His face is fruit complete with rot
as the blast goes through but leaves him
standing, as himself, comprised of ash.

When his whimper finally breaks,
a ring of light hides everything.

Counting Pebbles

He looks at people as he might count pebbles,
by the Brighton pier, in warm weather:
with this urge to keep each one discarded;
comprehending how he's not, in fact,
responsible—not now—for anybody
here. Families lay towels around: it's proof
in plenty of... well, of... he isn't sure.
He watches numbered couples on the verge
of gravel, at the rolling edge, whose hopes
of family go unspoken, yet... as yet...
but then, his thought dissolves into the swell.
For most part, it's the children: all the beach
awash with children, digging hands in water,
running them through stones; summer slipping
like a scream from slathered skin; the countless
voices, opened up to waves. And not
a single face among them noticeably
afraid. A silence separates him somehow—
drowning on the crowded promenade.
All this, he thinks, all this: it could be breath,
not simply sunken dreams for that small boy
(himself) who once drew smileys on the sky
to charm away the garden full with spiders,
gathering because, inside, two adults
yelled. The sound of breakers, or the calm,
                    made at the world's unravelling.

Headway

My powers stopped working
at the river.
Some of us had crossed

to the big stump but the current
beat my headway.
My powers never were for swimming.

I drifted to the weir
and did not bother the adults:

magic is to make things safe
without speaking.
A man stripped and dived.

I was hoisted on a towel
up a nettled bank. My skin
burned twice.

young woman views Chagall

at *Blue Lovers*, she is appalled
in a bright room, that storm colour
bruises her cotton suit
the shade of sloe

pictured: a face of static
lips nibbed, eyes closed

                    mother

it is not, in fact, paint's pressure
filling, but the nimbus
in her own chest
a wilderness, made numb

                    it is I

centre right: a muted harlequin
with stiffened ruff, the mask
a blot of dusk

                whom you clothed

the young woman touches her cheek
mimicking the gloved mime
who cups that of a widow

her mother's fascinator is neat
leaves, nature hemmed
indelible as hedgerow

                so I cannot speak

as though, in blackthorn
a spider wove her sack
to an iron pin
the young
never found the world

              these are my gauzed hands

the room bright, her suit
hoards shadows
tissue in a blue well

Westcountry Backwater

and the untruth of the suddengone
is pictured by homefolk
with boldface headline mouths;
in flashclips of settlements, wetlying.

It was all sawcoming.

Suchlike
as I foretold
an earthsink oncoming

when she cast me from kidhome
into a longschooling;
it was the dread-end arc
of her mother flounder

and I was thirteen aging.

Her lastgiven lesson
was to wordpour straight sentences
unlined; that, and the hyphen-
trick of wrapping runoff
round.

I have now a blindmind
for ink on rugfloor practice,
bedroom rain watching;
for her parentword, rising.

But its foreshadow still becomes.

Three decades done;
in some former thousand,
my teacher taught worldstop
science; ozone lens fear;
a hero's caring.

Had me flood mapbottom
contours in blue pencil,
prophesying archipelagos
of leftlying country crumbs.

And sure, as level home
under wave happens,
forebelieving is forgotten.
The looksee
hearsay warning lost
like the backnowing

of a child underswept.

Making Tracks

My lad leaves this khaki flatland leased
from the ocean. I watch him go.

He used to motor down this rutted drove,
burn through the broken club willow.

I could have told him, the moor is an in-breath
and submerges with a sigh. If I stopped him

a moment, he would key off the bike's rusty revs,
lean in its farm sack saddle, squint

under the day heat, to listen. I could have told him,
some tendon stretches the land inside us

fit to snap. It would not have mattered.
My lad leaves today, with a prickle

like a bed of withies, a breeze
in the hairs of his back.

Earth

Spelunking the Worldwide Web,
I pick at the touchpad, fingering a scar
of trees and dented earth, threaded

over Google Maps: a fault line
passes underneath the house
where I was born, fragments

sneaking, stagnant, where two crop fields
make a seam. Its humpbacks lift the lanes
across dry dumps of rusty coils

and fertiliser sacks. The lengthy barrows
are golf-course-smooth, beneath a rabbit paw
or cattle hoof. *Tap twice, zoom through.*

My claim is ancient. Once, I walked
this arc—from where the aqueduct,
half-sunken, crept between the rubble

of its parapet—then burst a bank
and stumbled on the tunnel
mouth: two lolling centuries of mud.

Where the line of clicks concludes,
I find three goons on a Flickr stream,
who tug a dinghy into that same arch.

Their head-beams widen a snakeskin corridor
and under the calcified dribbles
they thumbs-up for the shoot.

Brothers' Den

I revisited that bunker,
where he and I ran from fields
to a slab-nest base of *ack-ack*
and *ratter-tatter.* On its grenade-

stopping pillar were charcoal
genitals, drawn after someone's
lager-can-cracking fool-vigil.
Using an ember, I chalked

initials on the wall of this burrow
block. As the brook sucked
its stones like sloe berries,
water told ears what feet think.

And evening had kept grass's odour,
over which daddy-longlegs
scattered—their slapstick became
acrobatic in long blades.

That was how it felt to fit—
not be the jester on the precipice—
when dead concrete boxes could thrill
us; a broken edge hold us.

Tinnitus:Signal

(1:1)

Where I'm from he speaks in Zs and Xs telling me where the canal
went under—find the tunnel like honey-cells if you listen for the
pump running dok-dok-dok like a heart in your pillow, like a pit-
diggers' song.

Tinnitus:Signal

(1:2)

I cannot talk of childhood without helicopters and their judder of
Zs always overhead when I (the kid) push my Corgi cab on the
carpet stripes, hold a Decepticon (Lazerbeak) in the privet hedge,
run a nail down fake snow still turning black on my bedroom
glass, in (hummed) words forgotten between rotors.

Tinnitus:Signal

(1:3)

Night time hillside. Zap-lines in parallel converge on a metal
larch, big as. We children older, sparking upward but not saying,
not who hopes for who, even me. Cables above strum like
cellophane screwed in a fist.

N

For example, N, who is the first boy ever to do it
and is unlike all other boys, though N has been told

boys' bodies get ready soon, which is reasonable,
like new teeth or those hairs beneath his navel,

being automatic and so much a foregone conclusion
it has nothing to do with sitting here, pulling the skin,

hiding it, revealing, thinking perhaps there is this girl
whose face he cannot see, who keeps saying,

show me, show me, though why, he is not sure, nor who
she really is, only, the idea she wants to see is good, good,

repeatedly imagined—done—though she is hard to imagine
because girls do not say that, why would anyone (except

a boy like N who is unlike others) think of her saying it
as he shows her, over, feeling something, something new,

something like a gift opened, something like gratitude,
or a battery on the tongue, though not quite like waking

without air in bedclothes, knowing boys do not show girls—
who never ask—like N does now, as this lightbulb is crushed

into light and there is a flash, something hits him in the eye
and it stings, stings because she is gone, never there,

fading like a voice going *N, what have you done... done...*
a waking sickness, and never telling about an eye

glued shut, or a handful, almost yellow, though
he cannot know: it does not look that way a second time.

Alongside the Track

He shows me the spatter pattern, where once he spray-
tagged the depot brick. Brambles on a slipping bank
finger the handrail bolted to the wall. When a pigeon coos
from its crust of dung, I look up,
                                        to where a winch arm
juts like black gallows. Stencilled letters name this yard,
fading, four storeys above into the iron camber of the roof.
His hand reaches mine. Footsteps clanging on the stair.
We lean in, with daylight,
                                cobwebs gumming to my shins.
I've often thought of doing it in a place like this. But now
the floorboards stare back from mealy slits, and I've lost
my nerve. I can sense him, craning. Keen.
                                        Deep in the dim
and chalky air, an ancient engine swells under its lacquer,
glints with steam-gauge and wheel-spun valve. I look away,
to trace the cable rising, hatch by hatch, to the upper floor.

Closure

We duck the Securicor lens and cast a sly light onto flakegreen
radiators. Embered beams cross a hall touched with arson. If this
is how the world goes, like a hospital built to the plan of an
evening star, we arrived too young.

In its derelict heart we find a chapel filled with splintered pews.
Now, here is a room of framed beds and ringed curtains, ragged
with echoes, a flower vase tipped.

Through wired glass lies a blitz of battleship cabinets, a fly's
flicker on patient records. We wash the pastel bricks with our
torches. Pads unfold, crayoned for somebody's grandpa or niece.

Elsewhere, in cliques vested with power, there must be a man
who dismantles this institution ghost by ghost. Not us. If the State
leaves corridors to despair, we thrill for it.

Along the radials between clinics, let us paint that we were here,
stepping out over glass dust to a line of rusted wheelchairs, our
names across the ward doors, hyphenated by their swing.

Pieces of Litter From 1999

That year, my parents danced like fencers.
I found friends through music. We all did.
Psy-Trance was the ribcage thumped by muscle.
Chicken bones and onions fell to the kerb.

Love was an act with umbrellas and high wires.
I left the caravan while she stayed in Cornwall.
I clippered my head in case I was rumbled.
By winter, a man's blood caked the call box.

I showed my artwork in the shop—"anonymous."
My boss said to find a home should feel possible.
The couple next door were strangers who blamed me.
Battery acid splashed my only coat.

My father lived in a chasm, full of cash.
The phone box by the pool was where I called.
Those mushroom nights were loneliest of all—
I think green hair had suited me.

What a Piece of Work is a Man

Pencil me spreadeagled onto a circle, both cruciform
and starjump. Label around me branded toiletries

whose mention itself would be an advertisement—
divinity is within their form. Sketch along my arms

the ratio of muscle:fat that generates implicit threat.
People should think of gymnasiums and feel regret.

Each pocket of bared underfur must sweat colognes
of *brawl* and *toil*, qualities by which I provide for you.

Disguise these in more demure chemicals, bottled as sex.
Draw my chest in cutaway, half slogan v-neck, half

residual nipple that grants me privilege to hold forth.
Portion my stomach sixfold, so as to imply beverage

rather than egg box. Give me the legs of a chancer,
a marcher, jeans-ready, and haired. Between legs,

place my war-stopping heart, too terrible to depict
in public. Crown me lastly with my face, denuded.

Formation

A wasp on the cock is what I like.
Clasped in an eggcup on my testicle
until its creep lets me peak.

I was seven, and Saffron read at the wedding.
One crawled into my Y-fronts, but my blabber
got swatted by Mum's frown. I gritted and reddened.

She would sometimes buzz in her bedroom.
It is odd what the human voice still means
when devoid of face. Her little moan.

Saffron snickered with her schoolmates
as my skates slipped on a fool's pass.
We never kissed. A gold blazered doofus.

The brush of six legs takes me there.
When I finish, its feelers still fondle the jar.
The stash I keep hums. To get stung is rare.

That

It beggars
me, I did that to you.
That you... accepted. Said
nothing.

Should it have seemed
a different silence
to that which welcomed
a first kiss,
or said *unbutton this*?

What did I miss,
that time but not
another when my mouth
begged across your hips,
cautious right to that eventual,
certain yes? But I did

that to you. After,
we lay close
with a new trust,
a boundary crossed.
Nothing gross could mar
our need, just deepen it.

It took years
to tell me *it hurt*.
You hated it, wished

I would have stopped.
If we could go back
now I would beg you
to refuse.

Incidence:Reflection

If, in a bus station, two people (who will one day fall in love) sit opposite on red benches which fold like cinema seats, bus stations everywhere occupying, dropboxlike, these same coordinates in spacetime where each of us would know the same sparkling floor, remember the place gum is pressed behind pipes, or how all tiled walls are touched with dieselgrime and a crane fly endlessly expires in fluorescence, and if, because such halts are built to expel us, one of these two people (who are soon to fall in love) has sent his mind away to some peak with boulders and peat and melon-red grass, but the other, instead, only lopes his eyes, catching eventually the first's, so distant with falcons and mist he thinks his gaze is clasped, headlong, such that he smiles a surprised smile which melts through thought, to recognition, and if, suddenly, these two people (who begin to fall in love) find themselves spanning those dimensions without knowing whose long glance first lit whose, is it—on reflection— a mistake?

Clubbers

Acid vocal dissolves on kick drum
and figures kaleidoscope in the black light
fog and neon. Everybody has a smiley
on their mouth. We come here to move,
to sweat and to belong. In your mandala pupil
this isn't working, you're snake-

skinning yourself into a tube.
I pass you my water, brimming
with lasers and want to show you
how we emerge from our faces
as surely as the projector screen
fountains pixels from its empty centre.

Tinnitus:Signal

(2:1)

Let's purchase some cosmic at the herb doctor shop selling Hopi candle with his chart for the earway pilgrims' maze like a beeswax larva humming inside its valve.

Tinnitus:Signal

(2:2)

Meantime, the demons who chant rounds to me have heads like my tutors: *Get a move on, get a move on.* My neighbour petrol-strims the Kingdom Hall, neat borders whispering to him his final reckoning. I drop the acid, crossed on my rag rug.

Tinnitus:Signal

(2:3)

Here's what to think: a valve amplifier in a bloke's bedsit resonates cool. Something holy about sleeping in the room with your fridge.

Talking *Sense* With the Bloke With Fluorescent Labrador

He taps for bumpy slabs at the pelican crossing.
I want to pause him, work through my seers' guilt,
and tell him, "Listen to the siren pass, its *nee-nah*
dopplers to a *nee-naw*." Like fabric in a knee-sock

stretched thin, departing galaxies redshift
and we know the universe grows less blue.
No one sees that, everybody has eyes closed.
Science describes sound as air lapping at the earholes

like a cheeky tongue. They say matter
is basically a boy-racer's bass track
coming up through your soles, and light
in a vacuum resembles nothing: it has to thump

and bounce. Instead, I put my hand on his arm
to ask him if he once stretched the plastic binder
from four cans of beer against his lip, then pulled,
to feel *hotness* and *thinness* grow together, in proportion.

Neuroscience and Mycology in the Bedroom

There's me, under the big light with my belly
like a puffball. My chest hair makes shadows
downward like muscle. I can see my girlfriend
behind my reflection, our clock winks this instant.

She assures me my buttocks look good tonight.
But my brain is a mushroom, matted as pubic
hair below ground: mycelium to my fruit body.
It takes almost half a second for it to assemble

what the eye sees, each blink drifting like spores
along axons, into earth. Which means my face
right now is in the past, unknowable to me
as my arse. She says I should come back to bed.

Under the puffed quilt, our arms and legs
make nerve fibres that connect in a billion ways.
When our heads finally pop open and clouds
explode upward, we're just half a second apart.

Coming Up For Air

She makes him taste of tarragon,
olive oil, black pepper.
He does not rinse his beard.
He wants to wear it

into the warm street like a lit flume.
People gull around his wake,
scenting his beard
comb the line of hers.

A man with rolled sleeves
sniffs and wants to plunge
his tongue
but, through a window, a cab driver

draws breath, tasting
how he waited on
her nipple.
In the foyer, a clerk's hand

floats over keys,
watching lift-numbers
kiss up her ribs, back down.
The lift fills with pepper

and tarragon. He parts the way,
his beard glowing like her olive
glow, he licks spiced lips
and remembers: goes in.

The Plan

When old and rich, my love, let's spend
our last on cliffs, above the copper sea.

A whitewash house with windy slats and slates
that shake, its iron gutters rusted through.

Where you can plant us blue hydrangeas
that conduct the sky into the chalk,

and we might count away the teatimes
by the tussocks tumbling down to surf

as saltwind mouths away the lawn,
until our driftwood porch has gandered out,

a jawbone, jutting over circled gulls.
And this is when the night will plughole

at the crosshatch glow, beneath the highest eave,
and lightning sound the flintcrest heave and ho;

while you and I, at four a.m.,
thunder with the bedstead on the wall,

a bolt will plunge the flower bed,
the headland bitten like a scone,

and we'll crescendo to the ocean floor—
ride the rocksled through a whooping storm.

A Funk of Weather Turns

She chews the problem's stub, thumbs
her thunderhead, jotter open.

A patchouli stench of mould
blows off the kitchen curtain—

she shifts to the other elbow, palm
crooked. Netting parts to unmask

cloud-banks, lit like mustard
at last light. The pressure cooker

on the hob hisses mist; she twists
to check the knotted shelf, where

she keeps a clenched fir cone, hangs
bunches of crackled bladderwrack;

she savours graphite in her mouth
as she sums her workings out.

The rainfall is a pitter-patter
of mathematics. Vapour is raised

to the power of thunder. Net curtains
display calculator numbers

when a knife-and-fork flash cuts mustard
clouds to ribbons. Bladderwrack

slackens. She smells accelerating tyres

as the pinecone pops—the valve

rockets off the cooker. Convinced,
she slams down her pencil—

rough as chewed cob. The air prickles
with ozone and throbs with a funk

of stewed lentils. She spits out
the last splinter of stub.

Renovation

At first, his khaki-covered truck was a bed, parked beside the
    ramskull cottage.
He woke to absence, as if she vanished a second before. No
    cocoon of conversation,
only birdcalls breaking against canvas.

By day, he pulled millipede stems of ivy from stonework, sawed
    back the elder
in the kitchen to a stump, cored its roots with flame. He boiled
    wellwater clear
with her image, and stirred stew as he remembered.

Leaves began to circle when he hammered metal to church
    bone beams. The way
she used to save the sayings of lightminded thinkers until the
    fridge door was full—
a shelter over his own tumbledown words.

With burner finally snug in the rockfall hearth, he sat in the
    flaming dark,
its tongue on him, up from the groin. Her arms still ivy on his
    back. Rain gritted
against that roof, its tin flue tipped off kilter.

Betsy

Her man is a glass attraction, stacked with quids
and fivers; the promise of a heart's trove,
mechanically pushed to his lip. She has slotted
a pocketful of 2ps, hoping to find the knack,
a lucky tuppence—to hear that *chacka-chacka*.
Perhaps, on this next try, he will make change.

Flood

I saw rivers
go shapeless over banks
the day she went mad

and took pins
through photos personally
watched a microwave
like broken telly

but I believed in thawed ice
that a brass barometer
turned in her cells

shame
how I clung
to banks
with trees

Against Every Footstep

there is so much gravity.
The sun makes radials
through horse-chestnuts
and water courses like radio noise
from the weir. There is a roar
of flame, a smell of spent fuel.

My phone is silent at my ear;
the park is full of champagne voices.
A balloon with rippling sides
stretches lengthways on the grass,
a whale drinking in warmth.

Bottles clink. The wicker basket
is large as a van. I don't feel
any breeze. When I left you,
in the secure ward, the sob
you gave pegged me to the floor.
I put your mobile in your hand,

called you there, face-to-face,
kept talking through the swing doors
while a nurse held your arm.
The balloon finds its fullness now,
as though by surprise. Walks
by itself above the trees.

The Buzzing Crowd

Billy gives the rooks her murder face
and takes her tent and Sainsbury's bag
through undergrowth, beside

the carriageway. It's safe. A buzzard watches
traffic here some days. She's seen it
squall away, its nest

unknown, but Billy gets what it's doing.
She camps in bushes, crooning to
her dolls, and eats madeira.

She'll hop the fence to squat and bury tampons.
In the sky, rooks set upon
a buzzard, yelling, "Brat."

It screams, "Leave-you," and goes. Those rooks,
they'd peck your brain and pull love right
from out your sockets. When

two black-beaked men descend with crack-
ling caws, Billy screams at first
but has nowhere to go

except the home. She hides her dolls and tells
nobody what she's doing. She
watches the traffic, some days.

Sid is Material

Today, Sid is net curtain,
which is to say, he is flesh.

He steps from his doorstep
into light frost, as a man

billows into him, heading
for the launderette. The frost

is light, the man's duffle bag
only shines. Today, Sid

is flesh, which is to say,
he is bus ticket, frozen to kerb.

He passes the window where now
the bloke loads a drum

among turning drums. Sid is 80%
water, which is to say, machine

turning memory of pavement—
of peppered suds—of light to net

memory of flesh. Some days,
all Sid can do is remember.

He turns toward the bus stop,
mechanical, which is to say,

a line scored into glaze. Someone

taps his arm like white pepper,

asks if the number 10 just passed.
Today, Sid is bus stop signpost,

a shadow across the path.

Creep

Your carpet crawls like droplets on a hotplate
and the fear of tiny mouthfuls grows, exponential
to fleabites.

TV fizzes, and news is scroungers
piggyback our sweet creatures: the country
begins to flake.

You go outside, where dog walkers pointedly
claw at the dole office. Suspicion
crawls up you

as you back for home. Through the curtain,
every curtain on the street fidgets
like carpet fibres.

I Am Hive

after Jenny Diski

The pest guy was awkward,
said they aren't here. The doctor
recommended the pest guy.

The cream did nothing.
I shaved my body bald.
Burnt every outfit but this one.

I don't bother to scratch
now. We are like a family
secret, they and I.

Under the microscope
I must resemble pumice.
They flinch into follicles

when the light switch flicks.
By their feelers, I know them.
Textbooks never mention

this ecology. No one is telling.
Most likely, I'm their sole niche:
something specific in my grease.

Once, I closed a jar on one.
It vanished through the glass.
This cannot be called *crazy*,
my mind is the last thing mine.

Chloroform Hunger

I need the handkerchief to enfold
my mouth; life's ballet of faces
to melt. I want to swallow oblivion
like a scallop, whole—pinch thought
to a crescent nail. In this last split
of an eyelid, I can envision rooms
painted in uniform emulsion;
windows airtight behind white-
out blinds; spot-bulbs centred
over bathtubs of warm milk.
I crave tissue on my face, smelling
of printer paper hoarded without ink;
tablecloths set with sunwater
and cold cubes—to pull meat
like desert dunes from bones
of plaice. Before amnesia opens
its snowblind pupil, this snatch
at satisfaction: hunger, emptied
into a bottle and rag, the world faint
as mosquitoes over tundra.
When I hare toward ice.

Ventolin Reverie

On these sarcophagus nights,
thin sheets become hessian.
This strawdust breath
inspires the mind to scheme
over spirited oxygens.
—I am progeny of asphyxiation,
doing underwater widths
in the asthma-blue murk.

With clay boot for lung,
each spumy thought
synthesises
a thin harmonic,
while daybreak
—that brassy *klopfgeist*!—
gives a bathtub-knock
with my head submerged.

Perfectly alone in this
salt-hinged chest, I am
pinholed light
clamped awake
in breathy aspiration.
The body creaks
like sampled piano pedals
underdubbed to a thin score.

Tinnitus:Signal

(3:1)

This only boundary, so indistinct, at the faintest it is no line but the saw of an oscilloscope, hear: the superpositional fuzz behind space / the error in a shorted nerve, the same.

Tinnitus:Signal

(3:2)

Under wave, hear the drop which passed through all whales, what they thought of drill and rudder, and to lay back in bathwater is to listen to a planet named Ocean like a stadium poured into the ears.

Tinnitus:Signal

(3:3)

Loft of wingbeats, a headful of noise pollution and critiques of the lullaby: simply, *I hate the starling.** Give me, rather, three lanes of traffic, the perfect number of metres through a cracked windowpane, in whose sweet sussurus I may snore.

esp. at dawn

The Dammed

He could jolt
his depression, just
as a mountain was bored hollow
then stuffed with turbines
and a lake
is dropped through the mountain,
surging The Grid so a nation
may boil a lake of cups.

Then at night, the lake is wound
back up the mountain: effort
outweighing its gain in kilowatts.
Just as, at night, he tosses about
his own net loss, and he cups
his lake by drops.

Tarmac Blues

The pavement is a tar pool
to the man who treks home
on a blooming avenue
of horse chestnut.

His brick-laden eyes
stamp landmarks
to shorten the stretch:
some reddened railings;
a pillar box; *The Rose.*

His steps are long-
distance
haulage.

       Then it comes, the day
he peels back the road,
turns over miles
on an updraft, riding
the surface like a bike lesson

for the first time
without adult hand,
without stabilisers,
without *noticing.*

Homing on the Beacon

Soul is an echo, a word
like *length* or *weight*,
meaningless, except to talk
about one thing beside another.

Useless to explain what goes missing
on days when joy drops the pebble
down a caved stairwell.

One rattling phonic will not restore
whatever fills my person's
shape with something person-shaped.

And so I'll climb
toward a cable of hawthorn
frayed on the sky back,
a boulder infinite
with crystal;

I'll clamber
through scrub (purple)
to reach that cairn
whose position is absolute,
where the moor is all ways:

then pin my feet to the heap and fill,
solid as a parasail.

Lost for Looking

Every day, face flat to the glass ceiling,
resumés, bounced back by the mailer-dæmon;
knackered by hours trapped
inside telephone queueing systems.
Behind the brass plaques of financial wisdom
we find the *smack* of black pistons.

I have seen avid academics sidetracked
by speaker stacks and electric guitar rhythms,
or seek oblivion among people packed
in eclectic bars. Or search for religion
in the architecture of skyscrapers, in rays
from cracked prisms. Maybe we're driven
by some conception of a summit,
whether we climb a hard path
or ride cable cars, unable to establish
the essence of a single, truthful task?

One glass cubicle in sunshine's
all I ask—suspended crystal
illuminated like a music hall
or marble arch.

Stardom

He went to Trev's shed.
Rodents crossed barrels
in bare vinegar light.

Trev's whipped lurcher
paced its asylum cage.

Down the lane,
under the tin,
getting caned
on Trev's slop,
until two men with mugs
became the party
in a far city
he craved.

If the cosmos were fair,
no thirsty man
would have this fear of light.

But late, tripping
through the barn door,
he stepped around the lane
like it was a square stage—

performed within the spot
of townless stars.

I Swore I Would Never Shoot a Lighthouse

Today, you tell me you will die soon, jealous
of an old man dogwalking the dunes
who has mixed his bigotry with talk of coal ships
on that muddy straight.

It is late, the power station is an ice-cube
across the mica flats, and cider stymies us.
We have not reached the eyelid wreck; instead
you say it now, by the stilt-legged beacon—

lonely as a Tove Jansen sketch—
60, tipsy, and suddenly intent. I wonder
how a metal shack on limpet steps
survives on sand? I have a secret.

It will be she who goes, while you persist
in years of alcohol and stress. Across the water,
the plant is floodlit by a nuclear glow.
My camera out, I whir and click.

Die Back

Downpour. Over his ale,
he tells me, *Ash wood burns wet.*
Trains in disarray, villages
silenced. The English—
forever unprepared. To reach
a bus stop we needed waders.

That website showed us
how to spot the rot: patches
in bark like porter soaking
shirtsleeves; twigs'
black fingernails bared
above canopies.

We fought flash floods
on roads which closed like zips
behind us, to this inn fire
under these ceiling beams.
Some things appear changeless;
there are no tales of tomorrow.

Away in lanes, overhung by ashes'
banana-bunch branches, comes
a creeping flame. Another ale—
he tells me there were fewer
floods, back in his day.

Counsel of Alders

And now I go, to learn what alders show
in red coronas, by their tack-black skin,
through diagrams which ink December blues,
dissected hearts, unfolded into parts.

On liver-tinted lines, I'll glimpse
my insides with a coat of frost,
and know this means to *cease/*
begin/reside are of a kind.

Then stop there, my bisected limbs
unfolded ventricles, dark catkins
to the winter rays, and all I hold
within arrayed in wind.

Calling Collie

When man calls collie, they are fleet, they are swarm.
Curled in blanket till man's word—collie springs
hours into the second. If collie crosses underfoot, it means
world is mess of string. Collie hates man to be alone—
blood instinct ushers the herd. The path to quarry is rounded
because collie wants world to curve. Collie scents parallels
    in fields,

streets and moors. As man toils, collie works. Man
    pursues hobby
like world is collie's ball. Man forgets his own teeth, till collie
    shakes
his hand. When collie speaks words short
and long, world has to happen. Man meets collie's blue-
brown eyes... which of them makes up his mind?
Each day, man wakes differently; collie says world
    is unchanged.

Aknowledgements

Thanks go to the following colleagues, teachers, judges, editors, publishers and promoters, for their critique, validation and acceptance of these poems:

Andrew McDonnell (*Lighthouse*), Anna Saunders, Athena Dixon (*Linden Avenue*), Ben Banyard (*Clear Poetry*), Candy Bright, Carol Ann Duffy, Catherine Ayres (*Take Ten*), Charlotte Ansell, Claire Graham, Dr. Darren Richard Carlaw (*StepAway*), Emily Fay McCoy, Eve Anthony Hanninen (*The Centrifugal Eye*), Geoffrey Bailey, Hannah Linden, Helena Nelson, Ian Beech, Jan Fortune (*Envoi*), Jan Prior, Jane Burn (*The Fat Damsel*), Jane Commane (*Under the Radar*), Jenny Hill, Jinny Fisher, Jo Bell, John Murphy (*The Lake*), John Stuart, John Vick, Jon Clark, Julia Webb, Juliet Wilson (*Bolts of Silk*), Mark Totterdell, Martin Malone, Natalie Shaw, Paul Mortimer, Paul Tobin, Penelope Allen, Peter Oswald, Poppy Kleiser (*Poems for Peace*), Rachael Clyne, Rebecca Cleaver (*Blast Furnace*), Rebecca O'Conner (*The Moth*), Robert Harper (*Bare Fiction*), Roderick Bates (*Rat's Ass Review*), Rosie Sherwood (*Elbow Room*), Ruth McKee (*Spontaneity*), Ruth Stacey, Sam Smith (*The Journal*), Sarah James, Sarah L Dixon, Sue Kindon, Tom Sastry and Zelda Chapell (*Elbow Room*).

And to all others who gave voice to my work.

Gram Joel Davies grew up in Somerset in the '80s, overlooking the valley town of Taunton, the Quantock Hills and the edge of Sedgemoor. He was home-educated in a council house before attending a comprehensive in his early teens. When he left, his poetry came with him through years interspersed with other fixations—electronic music, theatre, artificial intelligence, inebriation, pop science...photography. His writing has appeared in magazines such as *Magma, The Moth, Envoi* and *Lighthouse,* and has received listings and commendations from Penelope Shuttle, Peter Oswald, Liz Berry and Carol Ann Duffy, among others. In 2014, he and collaboration partner Hannah Linden won the Cheltenham Poetry Festival *Compound* competition. He claims expertise in elusive identities, bending the senses and short-circuits of the human mind. Working with *Juncture 25* poets, he attends readings and festivals across the Southwest. He takes particular interest in editing poetry and likes to spend days exploring moors, ruins, galleries and power stations with his girlfriend. This is his first collection.

V.